Cows

Cows

Mary Ann McDonald

THE CHILD'S WORLD®, INC.

Library of Congress Cataloging-in-Publication Data
McDonald, Mary Ann.
Cows/written by Mary Ann McDonald.
p.   cm.
Includes Index.
Summary: Introduces the physical characteristics, behavior, and life cycle of cows.
ISBN 1-56766-375-3 (alk. paper)
1. Cows—Juvenile literature. 2. Cattle—Juvenile literature.
SF197.5.M33   1997
636.2—dc21   96-46139
CIP
AC

Photo Credits

COMSTOCK/COMSTOCK, Inc: 30
COMSTOCK/Art Gingert: cover
COMSTOCK/Jack K. Clark: 20
COMSTOCK/Gary J. Benson: 24
COMSTOCK/S. Chester: 15
Cosmo Condina/Tony Stone Images: 23
David F. Wisse/DEMBINSKY PHOTO ASSOC: 6
Joe McDonald: 9, 10, 29
Renee Lynn/Tony Stone Images: 19
Tony Stone Worldwide/Tony Stone Images: 13, 26
Tony Stone Images/Tony Stone Images: 2
William Muñoz: 16

On the cover...

Front cover: A *Limousin cow* stands in a pasture in England.
Page 2: A *Hereford* cow sniffs her calf.

Table of Contents

People raise many different kinds of animals on farms. Some farmers raise chickens or pigs. Others raise horses or sheep. Some farmers even raise unusual animals like ostriches and buffalo! But one of the most popular farm animals is the cow. Cows are very important because we use them for many things.

These *Holstein cows* are standing in a field early in the morning.

What Do Cows Look Like?

Cows are large animals with four legs and a long tail. When people are talking about more than one cow, they often call them **cattle**. Cattle is just another word for cows. People around the world raise many different kinds, or **breeds**, of cattle. Some breeds are white. Others are black, brown, tan, or red and white. Some breeds look different in other ways, too. Some breeds have longer hair or a hump on their backs.

This *longhorn* bull has beautiful brown patches.

Many cows have horns on top of their heads. The horns are hollow inside. They grow out of a bony base. The horn itself is made of the same material as your fingernails and hair. Most cows don't need their horns, so farmers often remove them. That is done when the cows are only a few days old.

This *Brazilian Brahman cow* has long horns.

What Are Male and Female Cows Like?

Male cows are called **bulls**. Most bulls have a short temper and can be grumpy or mean. Some of them can even be dangerous! Male cows that are being raised for meat are called **steers**.

Female cows are called cows. They have an **udder** that hangs under their bellies. The udder produces milk. Each udder has four **teats**, which look a little like fingers. Milk comes out of the teats, like water from a tap.

This hungry calf is drinking milk from its mother's udder.

Why Do People Raise Cows?

People raise cows for many different reasons. Dairy cows are raised to give milk. There are several breeds of dairy cows. *Holsteins* are the most popular breed. They are either black and white or brown and white. Holstein cows produce the most milk of any breed.

These holstein cows are eating on the farm where they live.

Beef cattle are raised to be used for meat. *Black Angus* and *Herefords* are two breeds of beef cattle. Beef cattle usually grow faster than dairy cows.

Oxen are even larger than beef cattle. These big, strong cattle were once used to pull heavy wagons and to plow farm fields. Today, most people use trucks and tractors instead. But in some parts of the world, farmers still depend on oxen.

These oxen are taking a rest after working hard.

What Are Baby Cows Like?

A newborn cow is called a **calf**. Calves stay close to their mothers for their first few months. The cows protect their babies and give them a special food—milk!

Milk is very important to young calves. It helps them grow quickly. It also helps keep them from getting sick. When the calves are about six months old, they begin to eat grass.

These little calves have different markings.

Cows and bulls eat huge amounts of plant foods. They love to eat grass and another kind of plant called alfalfa. They also like dried grass, which is called hay. Other favorite foods are grains such as oats and corn. Most dairy cows can eat 20 pounds of grain or 30 pounds of hay every day!

These cows are eating alfalfa.

Cows have a large stomach with four parts. The first part stores food as the cow is eating. A little while after it finishes eating, the cow brings the food back up. All it takes is one big burp! Then the cow chews the food for the second time. This is called chewing its cud. When the cud is swallowed again, it moves on to the other stomachs.

This cow is chewing its cud in a field.

Cows live in almost every country of the world. Most dairy cows are raised on farms. During the summer, dairy cows live and feed in large, grassy areas called **pastures**. Twice a day, the cows go to the barn to be milked.

Most beef cattle are raised on larger farms called ranches. In the United States, most ranches are found in the southern and western states. Animals raised on ranches wander free inside a huge area protected by a fence. Some ranches are as large as a city!

Most cows live in green pastures like this one.

Why Are Cows Important?

The cow is the most important of all the world's farm animals. Many things people use every day come from cows. Almost all of the milk we drink comes from cows. Cheese, ice cream, and yogurt are other favorite foods made from cow's milk. Even glue and paint can be made from milk.

This cow and her calf are eating grass.

But milk is not the only important thing people get from cows. Beef is an important food in many countries. Skins from cows, called **hides**, are also very important. They are used to make tough **leather** for shoes, purses, clothes, and other things.

Some people do not agree with raising cattle or other animals to use for their meat or skins. Instead of eating meat, they eat other foods like vegetables or pasta. Some people also try to wear clothes that are not made of leather.

This Brazilian Brahman cow is a beautiful white color.

Cows are very important in our lives today. Without cows, you wouldn't be able to pour milk on your cereal. You wouldn't be able to eat a burger at your favorite restaurant. You probably wouldn't even be wearing such sturdy shoes! So the next time you see a cow, remember to say "thank you"—because cows give us so much.

Some cows wear bells so that farmers can tell where they are.

Glossary

breed (BREED)
A breed is a special type of an animal. There are many different breeds of cows.

bull (BULL)
A male cow is called a bull. Bulls can be dangerous.

calf (KAF)
A calf is a baby cow. Calves drink their mother's milk when they are young.

cattle (KAT-tull)
Cattle is another word for cows. Many farmers raise dairy cattle or beef cattle.

hide (HIDE)
The hide of an animal is its skin. Cow hides are used to make many things.

leather (LEH-thur)
Leather is a tough material made from cows' skins. Leather is used for shoes, clothes, purses, and other things.

pastures (PAS-churs)
Pastures are large, grassy fields where cows live and eat.

steer (STEER)
A steer is a male cow that is raised for meat. Steers cannot mate or produce babies.

teat (TEET)
Teats are part of a cow's udder. Milk comes out of them.

udder (UH-der)
An udder is the part of a cow that produces milk. It hangs down from the cow's belly.

Index